YAMI YUGI

the official character & monster guide

by arthur "sam" murakami

SCHOLASTIC INC

New York Toronto London Auckland Sydney
Mexico City New Delhi Hong Kong Buenos Aires

Cover/Interior design: Rocco Melillo

ISBN: 0-7172-9909-0

12 11 10 9 8 7 6 5   6 7 8 9 10 11/0

Printed in the U.S.A.
First printing, April 2006

YUGI MUTO

PROFILE:

Birthday: June 4
Astrological sign: Gemini
Education: 11th grade
Favorite Food:
Hamburger
Least Favorite Food:
Pickled shallots
Lives: Above his
grandpa's game shop
Friends: Joey Wheeler,
Tristan Taylor,
Téa Gardner
Rivals: Seto Kaiba

ALL HE EVER WANTED WAS A FRIEND...

Yugi Muto was a shy high school student who loved to play games. Yugi's bashfulness turned him into a loner. All he wanted was a friend.

While traveling around the world, Yugi's grandfather found an ancient Egyptian artifact known as the Millennium Puzzle. No one in history had ever successfully assembled the Puzzle—not until Yugi, that is. After Yugi solved it, the Millennium Puzzle glowed blindingly bright. It infused Yugi with the soul of the ancient spirit housed within the Puzzle, and Yugi became Yami Yugi.

YAMI YUGI

The young and steely-eyed Yami Yugi is an extraordinary and confident duelist who fights the ultimate battle at the Shadow Games. But who is Yami Yugi?

The spirit confined within the Millennium Puzzle is the spirit of the ancient Egyptian Pharaoh that locked away the Shadow Games millennia ago.

Unfortunately, the Pharaoh has lost his memory and does not know how he saved ancient Egypt. If the Pharaoh doesn't get his memory back, how can he save Egypt from being destroyed again?

That's where Yugi comes in. With the Pharaoh by his side, the shy and introverted Yugi slowly learns to believe in himself. Yugi also finally has a great group of friends: the risk-taking Joey, his reliable sidekick Tristan, and Téa, the cheerleader of the crew. Together, they'll need to regain the Pharaoh's memory… but can they?

LET THE ADVENTURE BEGIN.

Yugi's journey begins dreadfully when Maximillion Pegasus, the creator of the Duel Monsters, kidnaps Yugi's grandpa. The only way for Yugi to secure his grandfather's release is to win the Duelist Kingdom tournament. The odds, however, are against the young duelist. Not only does Yugi have to defeat the world's elite duelists in order to challenge Pegasus, but Pegasus also has a Millennium Item of his own—the Millennium Eye. The Millennium Eye allows Pegasus to see into his opponent's mind and view the moves the opposing duelist will soon make.

After Duelist Kingdom, it's time for Seito Kaiba's Battle City Tournament, where losing a duel means losing your rarest card. Yugi and the Pharaoh learn that winning this tournament holds the key to unlocking the Pharaoh's forgotten memories. But the nefarious Yami Marik, and his pack of Rare Hunters, will make sure Yugi doesn't get a chance to win in the most dangerous set of Shadow Games yet.

If that's not bad enough, Kaiba's step-brother Noah interferes with the tournament and traps our heroes in a virtual world with no chance to escape.

At the end of Battle City, Yugi wins all three Egyptian God monsters, which are the most powerful monsters in all of Duel Monsters. Before Yugi can use them to get back the lost memories, the devious Dartz steals the Egyptian God monsters. With the monsters' power—and by using the stolen souls of duelists around the world—Dartz will resurrect Grand Dragon Leviathan, the behemoth that destroyed the legendary city of Atlantis.

After defeating Dartz, Yugi finally thought he could catch a breath, but no way. He has to compete in Kaiba's KC Grand Championship Tournament, an invitation-only challenge to become the new King of Games. But hidden among the competitors is someone who's out to destroy KaibaCorp and plunge the company into bankruptcy. But who?

UNLOCKING THE PAST

That may be enough adventure for a lifetime, but the greatest quest has only begun. The Pharaoh finally travels back in time to ancient Egypt and starts to learn what happened in his past.

How did Duel Monsters begin? Who created the Millennium Items? What was the great evil that the Pharaoh locked away? As the Pharaoh slowly discovers the answers, Yugi must call on his many monsters to win the ultimate Shadow Game to end it all. Turn the page to meet Yugi's monsters.

YUGI'S MONSTERS

Yugi has many powerful monsters, but his true skills lie in using his cards efficiently to maximize their potential. In Yugi's hands, every card is useful.

THREE EGYPTIAN GOD MONSTERS

Of all the creatures in Duel Monsters, there are none greater than the three Egyptian Gods. Pegasus created the Egyptian God Cards, but sealed them away because he was afraid of their immense power.

The three Egyptian God Cards are not only the key to uncovering the Pharaoh's memories, but they may also have helped defeat the great evil thousands of years ago.

SLIFER THE SKY DRAGON

Yugi won his first Egyptian God in the Battle City Tournament against the silent duelist Strings. Yugi deftly played his hand, forcing the mime to run out of cards. Slifer the Sky Dragon not only becomes more powerful as its owner's hand grows, but its second mouth emits a powerful shock that defeats its enemies once Slifer lands on the battlefield.

CARD STATS	
LEVEL:	10
Attribute:	Divine
Type:	Divine-Beast

CARD STATS	
LEVEL:	10
ATTRIBUTE:	DIVINE
TYPE:	DIVINE-BEAST

OBELISK THE TORMENTOR

The first time two Egyptian Gods faced each other was in the Battle City Finals. Yugi won Obelisk The Tormentor—the second Egyptian God—by defeating Kaiba using Slifer the Sky Dragon.

Obelisk the Tormentor can pummel his opponents with the always fearful Fist of Fate.

THE WINGED DRAGON OF RA

This mysterious monster has many different abilities. Marik formerly owned this monster. It can change forms—from a sphere to a phoenix—to unleash new and vigorous attacks, each one more powerful than the last.

CARD STATS

Level:	10
Attribute:	Divine
Type:	Divine-Beast

DARK MAGICIAN

If there's one monster to represent Yugi, it's definitely Dark Magician. Yugi and Dark Magician have a special bond formed long ago in the Pharaoh's Egyptian past. As the Pharaoh journeys through ancient times, the beginning of their teamwork becomes clear.

CARD STATS	
Level:	7
Attribute:	Dark
Type:	Spellcaster

CARD STATS

Level:	6
Attribute:	Dark
Type:	Spellcaster

DARK MAGICIAN GIRL

Dark Magician's sole disciple might by young, but her big eyes and flowing blonde hair disguises her innate magical talent. Her origins also lie in ancient Egypt where she had a special link with the Pharaoh.

Dark Magician Girl also played a huge role against Dartz when she brought Yugi to the world of Duel Monsters to meet the three Legendary Dragons.

EXODIA THE FORBIDDEN ONE

Easily one of the most powerful creatures in Duel Monsters, Exodia has a unique power. When all five pieces of Exodia are assembled, every enemy is obliterated.

Yugi used this monster to defeat Kaiba in their first-ever duel. However, in ancient Egypt, someone other than the Pharaoh was controlling this unstoppable monster.

CARD STATS	
Level:	N/A
Attribute:	Dark
Type:	Spellcaster

TIMAEUS

This legendary dragon aided Yugi in his fight against Dartz and his Grand Dragon Leviathan. Dartz was scheming to destroy Earth and the entire world of Duel Monsters—until Timaeus joined the battle.

Timaeus has the ability to join with other monsters to form powerful new combinations. He once teamed up with Dark Magician Girl to become Dark Magician Girl the Dragon Knight.

Timaeus is an honorable monster. When the Pharaoh sold his soul to the evil powers of the Orichalcos, Timaeus refused to work with him.

When Timaeus fights against Dartz, he transforms from a dragon into his true self.

Alpha, Beta, and Gamma are each powerful enough to unleash magnetic mayhem, but their true power is unleashed when they use their attractive conduction to form Valkyrion the Magna Warrior. With its honed blade and soaring wings, it flies to its foes and slices them to shreds.

ALPHA THE MAGNET WARRIOR

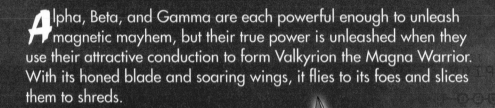

CARD STATS
Level:	4
Attribute:	Earth
Type:	Rock

BETA THE MAGNET WARRIOR

CARD STATS
Level:	4
Attribute:	Earth
Type:	Rock

GAMMA THE MAGNET WARRIOR

CARD STATS	
Level:	4
Attribute:	Earth
Type:	Rock

VALKYRION THE MAGNA WARRIOR

CARD STATS	
Level:	8
Attribute:	Earth
Type:	Rock

CARD STATS	
Level:	1
Attribute:	Dark
Type:	Fiend

KURIBOH

This cute and furry monster is one of Yugi's chief protectors, shielding the duelist from any monster attack. Kuriboh was a key monster in many of Yugi's victories against Pegasus and The Big Five.

CARD STATS

Level:	12
Attribute:	Light
Type:	Dragon

MASTER OF DRAGON SOLDIER

When eternal rivals finally decide to work together, great things can happen.

Against The Big Five, Yugi and Kaiba combined their forces instead of battling each other. They fused Yugi's Black Luster Soldier with Kaiba's Blue-Eyes Ultimate Dragon to form the almighty Master of Dragon Soldier.

B. SKULL DRAGON

Yugi and Joey's teamwork was put to the test in a tag-team duel against Pegasus's Paradox Brothers. The best friends passed the test when Yugi fused his Summoned Skull with Joey's Red-Eye B. Dragon. The result was the flame-spewing B. Skull Dragon, which defeated Gate Guardian.

CARD STATS

Level:	9
Attribute:	Dark
Type:	Dragon

SUMMONED SKULL

CARD STATS

Level:	6
Attribute:	Dark
Type:	Fiend

Zap! Summoned Skull electrocutes its opponents with painful blasts of lightning.

When Weevil's Great Moth was soaked in a magical mist, Summoned Skull electrocuted it into submission because nothing conducts electricity better than water. Even Yugi's Grandpa got into the act when he used Summoned Skull to rescue Téa and Tristan in the world of Capsule Monsters.

JACK'S KNIGHT, QUEEN'S KNIGHT & KING'S KNIGHT

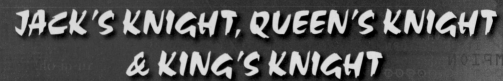

When Queen's Knight and King's Knight are together in battle, they gladly invite Jack's Knight to the party. With all three wielding their stunning blades, victory is in the cards.

CARD STATS

Level:	5
Attribute:	Light
Type:	warrior

CARD STATS

Level:	4
Attribute:	Light
Type:	warrior

CARD STATS

Level:	4
Attribute:	Light
Type:	warrior

CURSE OF DRAGON

GAIA THE FIERCE KNIGHT

GAIA THE DRAGON CHAMPION

This green monster has the ability to turn its opponents into charcoal. Gaia the Fierce Knight skewers his enemies by galloping into battle with its twin lances. Each one is powerful on its own, but when they combine to form Gaia the Dragon Champion, they're even more unstoppable.

Gaia abandons his horse to ride the dragon, combining flight, flames, and lances. Yugi used Gaia the Dragon Champion to burn the field against Weevil and set up his victory.

BIG SHIELD GARDNA

In battle, Big Shield Gardna is the monster you want at your side for protection. His oversized shield blocks powerful attacks.

CARD STATS	
Level:	4
Attribute:	earth
Type:	warrior

CARD STATS

Level:	4
Attribute:	wind
Type:	Dragon

WINGED DRAGON, GUARDIAN OF THE FORTRESS #1

This menacing creature spews fireballs, which Yugi used to his advantage in his duel against PaniK. PaniK's monsters were hiding in the shadows, so the fireballs lit up the darkness, and Yugi found out where his enemies were.

CARD STATS

Level:	6
Attribute:	Dark
Type:	Warrior

DARK FLARE KNIGHT

Against The Big Five, Yugi and Joey prove once again that their teamwork is the best in the game. Yugi fuses his Dark Magician with Joey's Flame Swordsman to form Dark Flare Knight.

MIRAGE KNIGHT

Was that an attacking monster, or was it all a mirage? When Yugi used Mirage Knight against The Big Five, they were totally confused.

CARD STATS

LEVEL:	8
ATTRIBUTE:	Light
TYPE:	warrior

DARK MAGICIAN KNIGHT

With its sword of steel and its conjuring abilities, Dark Magician Knight is an expert in swordsmanship and spells.

CARD STATS

Level:	7
Attribute:	Dark
Type:	Warrior

DARK PALADIN

Yugi created Dark Paladin by fusing his two most powerful monsters, Dark Magician and Buster Blader. This combination monster took down all of Kaiba's Blue-Eyes White Dragons in a single blow during the Battle City Finals.

CARD STATS

LEVEL:	8
ATTRIBUTE:	DARK
TYPE:	SPELLCASTER

MAGICIAN OF BLACK CHAOS

Fueled by the chaotic energies of the beyond, this spellcaster channels the power to blast a dark energy sphere at his opponents. He gave Pegasus fits during the Duelist Kingdom Finals.

CARD STATS

Level:	8
Attribute:	Dark
Type:	Spellcaster

DARK SAGE

Thousands of years of experience makes the wise Dark Magician even smarter, transforming him into Dark Sage. Yugi used Dark Sage to finish off Joey in the Duelist Kingdom Semifinals. That win led to Yugi's final clash against Pegasus.

CARD STATS

Level:	9
Attribute:	Dark
Type:	Spellcaster

CARD STATS

Level: 8
Attribute: earth
Type: warrior

BLACK LUSTER SOLDIER

Yugi can only summon Black Luster Soldier by using the Black Luster Ritual.

BUSTER BLADER

Watch out dragons. Buster Blader is your chief nemesis. Most dragons won't survive its wrath.

CARD STATS

Level:	7
Attribute:	earth
Type:	warrior

CARD STATS

Level:	4
Attribute:	earth
Type:	warrior

CELTIC GUARDIAN

This elf's stunning sword slashes all enemies that threaten Yugi. Yugi can always count on Celtic Guardian. They've worked together from Duelist Kingdom all the way to the world of Capsule Monsters.

CATAPULT TURTLE

This reptile doesn't care if you have a strong line of defense. It uses its catapult to launch its teammates and attack you directly.

CARD STATS	
Level:	5
Attribute:	water
Type:	Aqua

MYSTICAL ELF

She may not be powerful on offense, but her great defense power protects Yugi.

CARD STATS	
Level:	4
Attribute:	Light
Type:	spellcaster

BEAST OF GILFER

Beast of Gilfer is a terror on the battlefield, with a balanced attack and defense.

CARD STATS	
Level:	6
Attribute:	Dark
Type:	Fiend

BERFOMET

You don't want to get caught in this monster's arms—all four of them.

CARD STATS	
Level:	5
Attribute:	Dark
Type:	Fiend

CHIMERA THE FLYING MYTHICAL BEAST

Fused from Berfomet and Gazelle the King of Mythical Beasts, this two-headed monster charges, crunches, and stomps his foes.

CARD STATS

Level:	6
Attribute:	wind
Type:	beast

MAMMOTH GRAVEYARD

This monster may be all bones, but you still have to watch out for its tusks.

CARD STATS

Level:	3
Attribute:	earth
Type:	dinosaur

MASTER DUELIST

HORN IMP

One of Yugi's first monsters, the horn of this little imp can be a pain.

CARD STATS	
Level:	4
Attribute:	Dark
Type:	Fiend

FERAL IMP

Feral Imp emits lightning from its elongated horn to shock its enemies.

CARD STATS	
Level:	4
Attribute:	Dark
Type:	Fiend

BEAVER WARRIOR

Beaver Warrior is strong on defense. In battle, this sword-swinging warrior is an imposing foe.

CARD STATS

Level: 4
Attribute: earth
Type: Beast-warrior

SILVER FANG

With its claws and sharp teeth, this beautiful snow wolf can rip its opponents to shreds.

CARD STATS

Level: 3
Attribute: earth
Type: Beast

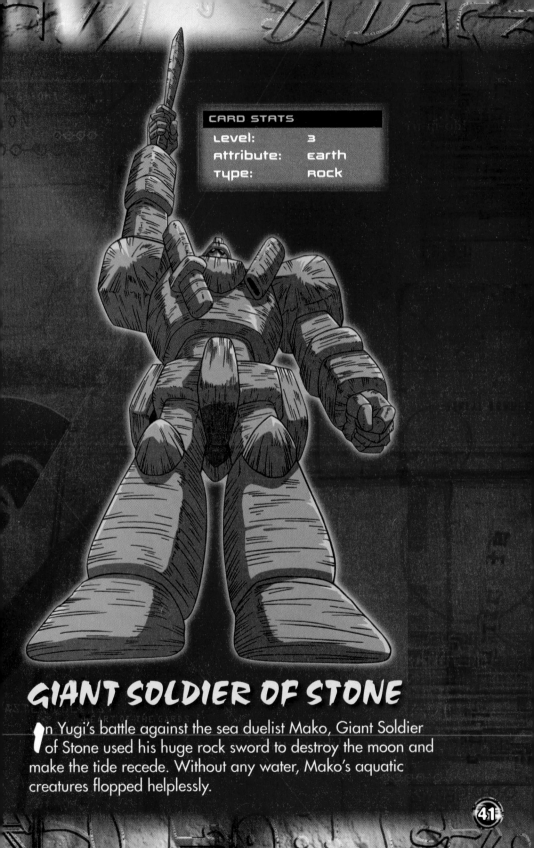

GIANT SOLDIER OF STONE

In Yugi's battle against the sea duelist Mako, Giant Soldier of Stone used his huge rock sword to destroy the moon and make the tide recede. Without any water, Mako's aquatic creatures flopped helplessly.

Yugi and Yami Yugi have summoned many monsters, but do you know the names of all their attacks and special abilities? If you know them all, you're a Yu-Gi-Oh! genius.

Monster	Attacks/Special Abilities
B. skull dragon	molten fireballs/ claws of flame
Black Luster soldier	chaos blade
Buster Blader	dragon sword
catapult turtle	launch catapult
celtic guardian	silverblade slash
curse of dragon	dragon flame
dark magician	dark magic attack/dark magic portal/rapid spell fire/ magical orb attack
dark magician girl	dark burning attack/ magical orb attack/ magical shockwave
dark magician + dark magician girl	double dark magic attack
dark magician girl the dragon knight	dark energy burst
dark magician knight	sword of dark magic attack

Monster	Attacks/Special Abilities
exodia the forbidden one	obliterate
mighty mage	lightning staff
feral imp	magic lightning
gaia the dragon champion	double dragon lance
gaia the fierce knight	spiral shaver
gandora the dragon of destruction	boundless gigarays
gazelle the king of mythical beasts	claw of destruction

Monster	Attacks/Special Abilities
Giant Soldier of Stone	Stone Splitter Sword
Griffore	Mythic Strike
Jack's Knight + Queen's Knight + King's Knight	Triple Majestic Slash
Kuribabylon	Horn of Chaos
Kuribee	Star Defense
Legendary Knight Critias	Sword of Wisdom
Legendary Knight Hermos	Sword of Renewal/ Sword of Freedom
Legendary Knight Timaeus	Sword of Justice/ Full Shield Barrier
Magician of Black Chaos	Chaos Scepter Blast
Magician's Valkyria	Mystic Scepter Blast
Master of Dragon Soldier	Dragon Sabre Blast

Monster	Attacks/Special Abilities
obelisk the tormentor	Fist of Fate/Fist of Fury/ Titan Firestorm
obnoxious celtic Guardian	celtic Blade slash Attack
Queen's Knight	majestic sword swipe
silent swordsman	silent sword slash Attack
slifer the sky Dragon	Thunderforce Attack/ Lightning Blast
sorcerer of Dark magic	celestial Blast
stronghold the moving Fortress	steel Gear crush
summoned skull	Lightning strike
The winged Dragon of Ra	Blaze cannon
Timaeus the Knight of Destiny	sword of Justice
winged Dragon, Guardian of the Fortress #1	Fireball Attack

Do you know when each monster first appeared on Yu-Gi-Oh!?
Test your knowledge against this chart.

EP#	Episode Title	1st time monster was summoned
1	The Heart of the Cards	Winged Dragon, Guardian of the Fortress #1
		Gaia the Fierce Knight
		Beaver Warrior
		Dark Magician
		Exodia the Forbidden One
		Horn Imp
2	The Gauntlet is Thrown	Koumori Dragon
		Silver Fang
		Celtic Guardian
		Summoned Skull
4	Into the Hornet's Nest	Mammoth Graveyard
		Feral Imp
		Griffore
5	The Ultimate Great Moth	Kuriboh
		Curse of Dragon
		Gaia the Dragon Champion
7	Attack from the Deep	Giant Soldier of Stone
10	Give Up the Ghost	Mystical Elf
15	Winning Through Intimidation	Catapult Turtle
21	Double Trouble Duel - Part III	B. Skull Dragon
30	Duel Identity - Part II	Black Luster Soldier
34	Best of Friends, Best of Duelists - Part II	Dark Sage
39	Yugi vs. Pegasus: Match of the Millennium - Part IV	Magician of Black Chaos
45	Legendary Heroes - Part III	Master of Dragon Soldier
56	Yugi vs. Rare Hunter - Part I - Battle City Begins	Beta the Magnet Warrior
		Berfomet
		Gazelle the King of Mythical Beasts
		Chimera the Flying Mythical Beast

DID YOU KNOW...

...that Joey and Tristan used to bully Yugi? When Yugi protected them from an even bigger bully, Joey and Tristan learned the error of their ways and became the best friends anyone could ever have.

...that Yugi is more than a Duel Monsters champion? He's also an expert in other games, including Capsule Monsters and Dungeon Dice Monsters.

...that Joey's Time Wizard first belonged to Yugi? Yugi gave Joey the card on their way to Duelist Kingdom as a sign of their friendship.

...Exodia the Forbidden One is one of Yugi's most powerful monsters, but he only summoned it once. Weevil made sure he could never summon it again by throwing Yugi's Exodia cards into the ocean.

...Yugi used to wear his Millennium Puzzle on a rope necklace, but he changed it to a chain necklace to make sure no one can steal it.